CU00847548

ANGEL
*The Ne*

Angela Topping is a freelance poet with twenty years
experience as an English teacher. She was Head of Lit-
eracy and Oracy at Upton Hall School until 2009. Her
poems have been widely published, are used in verse
speaking festivals all over the world, and feature in text-
books and on the internet education sites of various
organisations including Amnesty International and
Oxfam. Her work has been selected for use by The
Samaritans and The Open University in educational
resources, and also appears in examination anthologies.
She is a seasoned poet-in-schools for The Poetry Soci-
ety and Windows Project, Liverpool. She has mentored
many young writers and has tutored creative writing
courses for all age groups. Her poems have been per-
formed in a wide range of venues including The
Greenbelt Festival, Manchester Poetry Festival, and
The Bluecoat Arts Centre Liverpool.

Also by Angela Topping

*Dandelions for Mothers' Day* (Stride 1988
and 1989)
*The Least Thing* (editor, Stride 1989)
*Making Connections: A Festschrift for Matt Simpson*
(Editor, Stride 1996)
*The Fiddle: New and Selected Poems* (Stride 1999)
*The Way We Came* (bluechrome 2007)
*Focus on Spies by Michael Frayn* (Greenwich
Exchange 2008)
*Focus on The Bloody Chamber and Other Stories by
Angela Carter* (Greenwich Exchange 2009)

# ANGELA TOPPING

## The New Generation

CHILDREN'S POETRY LIBRARY
No. 4

SALT

LONDON

PUBLISHED BY SALT PUBLISHING
Dutch House, 307–308 High Holborn,
London WC1V 7LL United Kingdom

First published 2010

Printed in the UK by the MPG Books Group

Typeset in Oneleigh 11 / 14

ISBN 978 1 84471 765 1 paperback

1 3 5 7 9 8 6 4 2

*To my husband Dave, my daughters Laura
and Rosie, and members of Upton Hall School
Writers' Club*

*'Encourage youth and it will blossom.'*
Celtic Proverb

# CONTENTS

*Acknowledgements*                                     xi

Witch in the Supermarket                                I
Baba Yaga and Katie Weir                                2
A Wizard Teacher                                        3
The New Generation                                      5
Aunt Jane                                               6
Mer-Mum                                                 8
Midsummer Night                                         9
My Old Man                                             IO
Satanic Supplies                                       II
They Mean Business                                     I2
Dear Spider,                                           I3
Cat's Prayer                                           I4
The Prayer of the Rabbits                              I5
Counting Sheep                                         I6
Creatures Haiku                                        I7
Fears                                                  I9
Snake                                                  2I
The Pigeon Fancies                                     22
Rivals                                                 23
Savoy Hotel Cat                                        24
It's True                                              26
Teachers These Days                                    28
The Mean Librarian                                     30
To Be Chanted Very Loud at Playtime                    3I

| | |
|---|---|
| Classroom Hamster | 33 |
| End of Term Reports | 35 |
| Snitch | 36 |
| Not To Blame | 37 |
| Lonely | 39 |
| My Pets | 40 |
| New Start | 42 |
| The Staff | 43 |
| After School Cinquains | 44 |
| Bonfire Night | 46 |
| Hallowe'en Party | 47 |
| Christmas Tree | 49 |
| Recipe for a Festival | 50 |
| Recipe for a Birthday | 51 |
| The Creation Disco | 52 |
| Winter Morning | 53 |
| Weatherings | 54 |
| Finding Magic | 55 |
| Haiku for the Seasons | 57 |
| Friends | 58 |
| My Best Friend | 60 |
| After the Earthquake | 61 |
| Change Our Ways | 62 |
| Kenning My Dad | 63 |
| Riddle | 64 |
| Hypocrites | 65 |

After the Match                          67
Little Houses                            68

# ACKNOWLEDGEMENTS

Some of these poems appeared for the first time in the following anthologies:

*The Bees Knees* (Stride 1990), *The Bees Sneeze* (Stride 1992), *Can You Hear? Poems for Oxfam* edited by John Foster (Collins 1992), *We Was Robbed* chosen by David Orme (Macmillan1997), *Unzip Your Lips* edited by Paul Cookson (Macmillan 1998), *Spotlight on Poetry* (Collins 1999), *Teachers' Pets* chosen by Paul Cookson (Macmillan 1999), *The Upside Down Frown* collected by Andrew Fusek Peters (Wayland 1999), *The Works* chosen by Paul Cookson (Macmillan 2000), *Jenny Kissed Me* compiled by Fred Sedgwick (The Questions Publishing Co. 2000), *The Moonlit Stream* compiled by John Foster (OUP 2000), *Ready Steady Rap* collected by John Foster (OUP 2001), *Moondust and Mystery* chosen by John Foster (OUP 2002), *What Shape is a Poem?* (Macmillan 2002), *101 Favourite Poems* compiled by John Foster (Collins

2002), *Will There Really Be A Morning?* compiled by Fred Sedgewick (David Fulton Publishers 2002), *I Remember I Remember* edited by Brian Moses (Macmillan 2003), *My Stepdad is an Alien* chosen by David Harmer (Macmillan 2003), *Who Rules The School Now* compiled by Paul Cookson (Macmillan 2003), *Spectacular* chosen by Paul Cookson and David Harmer (Macmillan 2004), *Sensational* chosen by Roger McGough (Macmillan 2004), *Read Me and Laugh* chosen by Gaby Morgan (Macmillan 2005), *Trick or Treat* chosen by Paul Cookson (Macmillan 2005), *The Poetry Store* chosen by Paul Cookson (Hodder 2005), *The Universal Vacuum Cleaner* compiled by John Foster (OUP 2005), *Best Friends* chosen by Fiona Waters (Macmillan 2006), *The Works 5* chosen by Paul Cookson (Macmillan 2006), *Read Me Out Loud* chosen by Nick Toczek and Paul Cookson (Macmillan 2007), *The Elements on Poetry: Poems about Earth* chosen by Andrew Fusek Peters (Evans Bros 2007).

'Baba Yaga and Katie Weir' and 'Rivals' were first published in *Dandelions for Mothers' Day* (Stride 1988).

# WITCH IN THE SUPERMARKET

There's a witch in the supermarket over there
after Fowler's treacle for her flyaway hair,
buying up nail-varnish — black or green?
Rooting in the freezer for toad ice-cream!

There's a witch in the supermarket next row on
asking where the Tinned Bat's Ears have gone,
mutters, 'Why do they always change things round?
Mouse Tails and Rats' Tongues can't be found!'

There's a witch in the supermarket down that aisle
searching for something to blacken her smile.
She's a trolley full of tins for her witch's cat
who simply swears by Bit-O-Bat.

Times are difficult and Bovril has to do
instead of newt's blood for a tasty stew;
sun-dried bluebottles crunchy and sweet,
desiccated spiders for a Hallowe'en treat.

There's a witch in the supermarket at the till
scribbling her cheque with a grey goose quill!
There's a witch at the checkout, look, mum, quick!
Piling up her shopping on a big broomstick!

# BABA YAGA AND KATIE WEIR

And I must play the witch for them again,
cackle a croaky voice that makes me sore,
stretch fingers into bony claws to beckon with.
No one can do it quite like me. I act,
enjoy their screams when I pursue.
They're letting me join in, and for a change
it's me against them. Success is brief —
their stronger magic, longer legs outwit.
I'm left to bite on this — the thought
of that sour old woman's house
they always cross the street to pass.

# A WIZARD TEACHER

Mr McAlpine's a wizard!
I know 'cos I saw an owl
staring out of his window
when I passed by his house.

Those funny books he carries
walking round the school —
well, I caught a glimpse of one title
WIZZOGOGIGOOLE.

His hair's done in a ponytail.
My dad thinks that is weird.
He's got very bushy eyebrows
and a wizzy fizzy beard.

The gnomes he has in his garden
move around from day to day
sometimes they're all in a huddle
and you can hear the things they say

moaning about Mr McAlpine
and the work he makes them do.
They should try his number work —
it's the hardest in the school.

I quite like Mr McAlpine —
he knows how to tell a good tale.
He's told the class about Merlin
and knights that wore shiny mail.

He says that in the summer term
we'll all go on a trip
and see the cave at Alderley Edge
where King Arthur lies asleep.

I pity the other poor teachers
they really can't compete
with Mr McAlpine the wizard
when he magics us a treat.

# THE NEW GENERATION

Wizards look like everyday folk
despite what you've been told.
We don't have long white whiskers
nor are we very old.

We don't go round in trailing robes
except on special days;
those pointed hats are stylish
but out of the usual way.

We don't wear silver stars and moons
embroidered on our clothes;
we never wear those pointy shoes
they're murder on the toes.

I like to wear my Levi's,
roar up and down the street
on my Ducati motorbike,
Doc Martens on my feet.

I'm part of a new generation
of wizard girls, we're cool!
No one dares to mess with me.
Female wizards rule!

# AUNT JANE

My Auntie Jane is a funny old stick:
She's been alive for ever.
She likes to wear a long black dress,
a hat with a raven's feather.

Her skin is pale like marble,
her teeth are gleaming white,
her eyes are hard to fathom
She'll go out only at night.

She chooses crimson lipstick,
pointed shoes upon her feet,
her hair is swept up high.
I've never seen her eat.

I'm not allowed to visit her
without my mum and dad:
she has some quaint old habits:
my friends think she is mad.

Her house is quaintly spooky.
It's old fashioned, dark and cold.
She hugs me very tightly,
I can't escape her hold.

She always keeps the curtains drawn
and does not like the light,
there's not a mirror to be seen
for she claims she looks a sight.

She tells me how she loves me
she'll eat me up, she cries,
what pointed teeth my auntie has
what terrifying eyes!

My parents say it's time to go
and wrap me in my coat
they take such special care to tie
my scarf around my throat.

They say Aunt Jane's eccentric
and is better left alone
with her spooky castle of a house,
her bed carved out of stone.

# MER-MUM

She holds a silver-backed mirror
as she brushes her long dark hair.
Her sea-green eyes grow hazy
as she croons a mournful air.

She likes to swim in the ocean
every day when I'm at school
and in the summer evenings
she rests in the goldfish pool.

She wears her pearly earrings
her skirts fall to the ground
and as she glides along the floor
the scent of seaweed's all around.

I love my mermaid mummy
and I know that she loves me.
I dread the day that she decides
to go back to the sea.

# MIDSUMMER NIGHT

Madness, my nan says.
But I want to go
out in the dark
looking for fairies.

I'm sure they'd
come when I call
or if I tiptoe
I might just

catch them at
their revels
dancing in a ring.
I know where

the ring is.
Grandad told me
to watch where
bluebells grew.

# MY OLD MAN

My old man's a pilot.
He steers a big starship.
He wears white plastic trousers
and his food comes through a drip.

My old mum's a robot.
Her joints are made of tin.
She's covered with washable velvet
and she answers to the name of Lyn.

My teacher's a dalek.
He has a boring voice.
He likes to wave his wand at you
and exterminate the boys.

My sister's an alien.
Dad found her growing on Mars.
She won't touch peas and carrots
'cos she lives on chocolate bars.

My friends think I'm peculiar
because my ears are green.
If they saw what I turn into
they'd scream and scream and scream.

# SATANIC SUPPLIES

Live toads
Slimy livers
Crossroads
Blood givers

Velvet bats
Pilots' thumbs
Pointed hats
Mouldy crumbs

Grimoirs
Salted leeches
Eyes in jars
Skin of teachers

Broomsticks
Wart creams
Candles — black wicks
Recorded screams

*Orders made over the net*
*The best supplies you'll ever get!*

*Find us at: www.otherworld@rhymes.com*

# THEY MEAN BUSINESS

Better beware on the London Tube
for in amongst the crowds
disguised as office workers
are sinister beings in bowler hats.
Inside their leather briefcases
their wands are folded up.
Those files of accounts and orders
are really wicked spells
encrypted in numbers.
On their laptop computers
they contact other wizards
and conspire over plans
for world domination.
They mean business.
Look at their shiny shoes!

# DEAR SPIDER,

Thanks for the invitation
to your cosy dinner for two.
I'd really love to come
but I can't think what to do.
I can't decide just what to wear
my clothes are all so fine
and I'm not certain where to find
a suitable sort of wine.
I'm not used to dining out,
it's really not my thing.
I tend to snatch my meals
when I am on the wing.
My mealtime conversation
is limited in kind.
In short I feel that
I really should decline.
It's not that I don't like you
but we are so far apart;
I can't see it working out
although you want my heart.

Yours sincerely,
Fly

# CAT'S PRAYER

Dear Whiskered Lord,
thank you for your creation of birds
(but why did you give them wings?).
Thank you for mice and the human
who gives me food when I'm too tired
to go hunting. Thank you for milk.

And now I've praised you I can ask
let there always be milk and warmth
and these daft humans for servants.
Keep back the dog who barks and
anything that might spoil my slumbers.
In the name of fur, Amen.

# THE PRAYER OF THE RABBITS

Hail human, full of treats
water is with you.
Blessed are you among rabbit mothers
and blessed is your warm hand
when you stroke us. We like it when you croon
soft songs to us.
Take us not to the vets with her sharp needles
but bring us hay forever and ever.
Amen.

# COUNTING SHEEP

Sleepy, dozy, dropping off
on the pillow's down.
Nodding, blinking, yawning
gently carried off.
Rocked in mother's arms
with rhythmic lullabies,
fluffy pink pyjamas
softly closing eyes.
Cosy mound of coverlet,
hot water bottle sheets,
time to snuggle down
sleepy sleep sleep sheep.

# CREATURES HAIKU

### HAIRY CATERPILLAR

Wriggly and tickly,
I'm someone's missing eyebrow
scavenging for treats.

### LADYBIRD

I found a button
on a plant but it wouldn't
stop to be sewn on.

### SILVERFISH

Prehistoric things,
antique shiny silver things
how have you survived?

## BUMBLEBEE

Why do you bumble?
Are you unsure what to do
in your stripy suit?

## SPIDER

I don't like you; you
make me all tickly inside.
Don't scuttle like that.

# FEARS

I'm not scared of spiders.
I'm happy to handle a worm.
It's not quite true what Liam says
I'm not the sort to squirm.

I didn't cry out 'Help me'
when a moth came in the house.
Don't believe what Liam says
about when I saw the mouse.

I'm not keen on daddy-long-legs
but I don't make a fuss.
Don't ask me why Liam thinks
his mum is such a wuss.

He's got a pet tarantula
and scorpions in a box,
but I can cope with worse things —
like the smell of Liam's socks.

So don't believe a word of it
It's just a pack of lies
I am the greatest advocate
of everything that flies.

*Liam, Help! Your lizard's loose again*
*it's sitting on the cooker and I can't cook the tea!*
*Come on Liam for goodness sake*
*take the horrid thing away from me!*

# SNAKE

Snake
Tessellated
Oiled smoother
Sliding S
Shapes along
Wiggly tickly
Warm to the touch
Pointy-tongued
Clever old
Snake.

# THE PIGEON FANCIES

I watch the match every week.
Best view, for free.
Where I am I can see every player
and the waving crowd.
Sometimes, I stay up high,
squawking at dots of heads
chanting me own sweet chants;
other times I swoop right down,
hear the smack of boot meeting ball.
Could spoil everything if I wanted
by tangling them up with feathers and beak.
As it is I award me own 'man of the match'
by painting a white stripe on the head
of whoever played the best.

# RIVALS

She freckled custard, six eggs rich
with cinnamon, cooled it on pantry sill;
at tea-time found licked-clean pastry,
a smug cat washing in the gloom.

The lorry that he flung it on
was thundering to Manchester.
He cycled back to find the cat
slunk behind a chair, home first.

He chucked its hateful softness
onto a wagon with a Scottish name;
room cleansed of stalking cat
enjoyed his tea in peace at last.

Cat was too crafty to go back there.
It arrived at his factory next day,
tail and whiskers twitching, nosing his scent,
facing new boundaries, lying in wait.

# SAVOY HOTEL CAT

*The famous London hotel employed a cat who was
brought to the table to make up numbers whenever
thirteen people were sharing a table.*

I am the cat, the ebony cat,
I'm neat and smart, though I don't wear a hat.
I grace your table, chic and serene
when the number of guests is unlucky thirteen.

The Savoy Hotel knows a black cat's best
to be a superior dinner guest.
I relish my smoked salmon and cream
when the number of guests is unlucky thirteen.

I wear a napkin round my throat
to help preserve my glossy coat
for it doesn't quite do to be less than clean
when the number of guests is unlucky thirteen.

The ordinary kitchen cats show me respect
for it's known my manners are fully correct —
my impeccable behaviour's a treat to be seen
when the number of guests is unlucky thirteen.

I've entertained the aristocrats in my prime,
heard many a fine tale on the old grapevine

I've even graced the table of the queen
when the number of guests is unlucky thirteen.

These human creatures are a puzzle all right
it seems it spoils their appetite —
they can't enjoy this fine cuisine
when the number of guests is unlucky thirteen.

# IT'S TRUE

I don't believe yer.
*It's true, a big hairy one.*

Geroff, you'd hear it.
*Some have, screeching at night.*

But what does he feed it?
*The lines of those kept in at break.*

No bird would eat those.
*Who said it was a bird?*

You did.
No, I never. There's other things

*than birds go screeching at night.*
*It makes its nest in chalk dust.*

Now I know you're fibbing.
*I'm not, actually.*

OK, then, why has no one ever seen it?
*Some have, shifting from foot*

*to foot in the stock cupboard.*
Have you?

*No. But I dare you to go.*
No way. I don't care what

sort of animal that is, there's no way
I'd try and look in that stock cupboard.

You know what sir's like.
We'd better get these lines done

before the bell goes.
*I must not witter on in class.*
*I must not witter on in class.*
*I must not witter on i*

# TEACHERS THESE DAYS

*What are your teachers like?*
Bone idle, same as usual,
keep forgetting their red pens.
If they turn up again
with all the old excuses
as to why they haven't done their marking
they're going on detention.
Who do they think I am?
I wasn't born yesterday!
The dog ate it, indeed.

What about yours?
*Well, not too bad, though a few*
*are still not catching on*
*to the rules about uniform.*
*Those hoop earrings are just not safe.*
*I've had to confiscate loads of them.*
*And the gum! It's chew chew chew.*
*Yesterday I caught the head*
*sticking some under the table in the library!*
*Disgraceful.*

I know! Teachers these days.
They just don't try.
And another thing—

they've got no imagination.
It's terrible, this job.
And they are so ungrateful.

# THE MEAN LIBRARIAN

The mean librarian
gives us dirty looks,
makes us wash our hands
before we touch the books.
Hates us coming in,
says we make a noise.
thinks we can't read
says 'Books are not toys'.
She stamps out our books
like she's stamping on our toes.
Always says, as if we wouldn't,
'Take good care of those'.

The mean librarian
checks in our returns.
Looks inside them carefully
for crumbs and stains and burns.
Slaps them on the counter
as if she's slapping faces
then takes care to put them
in proper numbered spaces.
The mean librarian
will only be satisfied when
all the books are safe on shelves
and never borrowed again!

# TO BE CHANTED VERY LOUD AT PLAYTIME

Boys are mean, they pull hair.
Teachers are mean, they don't care.
Bullies on the playground
make you want to run
make you want to cry
but you can't tell your mum 'cos . . .

Mums are mean, they brush hair
you scream loud , they don't care
they make pigtails boys can pull
with big bows on so boys make fun.

Who needs mums, who needs dads?
Who needs boys, they're so bad?
Friends on the playground
make you want to skip
make you want to sing
and you want to pull your tongue 'cos . . .

Boys are mean, we don't care
Stick our noses in the air.
Girls are best, cute and funny.
We grow up to be boys' mummies!
We'll smack them and send to bed
get them back for the things they said.

We'll teach them to yank our plaits,
see how they like having smacks.
Boys are mean, they pull hair.
Teachers are mean, they don't care.

# CLASSROOM HAMSTER

I'm a classroom hamster
loved by all
even the caretaker
*that* grouseball

I love all the children
except that Timmy Green
whenever I can I bite him
I like to make him scream

My favourite one's the teacher
she brings me lovely food
she's always happy and cheerful
never in a mood.

I wish I was a pupil
playing in the yard
doing all my sums so neat
be sure I'd try so hard

to always use a ruler
the proper colour pen.
And when I'd finished all my sums
I'd do my writing then.

Instead I am a hamster.
I have my work to do.
I am a cardboard shredder
with my fantastic chew!

# END OF TERM REPORTS

Pinocchio's been lying again.
He's such a naughty boy.
He will not do his work
and seems determined to annoy.

Snow White's been good as usual
the Home economics prize
goes to her for the second time
for excellent apple pies.

Sleeping Beauty's had a bad term —
she can't stay asleep at all.
Cinderella's fallen out with her
for wanting to go to the ball.

Jack's failed Biology again —
his beanstalk fails to flourish.
He's developed a fear of giants.
He must work on his courage.

Parents' evenings will be held
a week next Tuesday night.
Please return the tear off slip
Yours, Mrs Everight.

# SNITCH

Long hair always pinched back
socks long white and lacy
always pulled up to the knee,
exactly level on each leg.
Long fingers that pinch
when no one is looking.
*She* never gets caught!
Hand is always up, waving,
'Oh *please*, Miss'.
She's the monitor, wipes
the board, gives out the books,
carries teacher's bag.
She totes a mean rubber
to exterminate imperfect letters.
Her birthday presents are better
than everyone else's.
She hangs out with other snitches.
Her favourite threat is *I'm telling.*
No one likes her, little Miss Perfect,
not even the teacher.

# NOT TO BLAME

It wasn't me! It's not my fault.
I wasn't even there.
I wasn't in the classroom
to stick chewy on that chair.

I didn't drop that litter.
I didn't spill that drink.
I don't do anything like that
no matter what you think.

I didn't cheek the teacher
I didn't answer back
that's not my paper aeroplane
I haven't got the knack!

It wasn't me! It's not my fault.
I wasn't even there.
I'd never write graffiti
and I don't even swear.

I never put a foot wrong
or get into any fights.
It cannot have been me at all
who left on all the lights.

It's most unfair to put the blame
on innocent little me.
If I did I don't remember
or hoped no one would see.

It wasn't me! It's not my fault.
I wasn't even there.
Why do I always get the blame?
Life is so unfair.

# LONELY

I've got no friends
it's sad for me.
At playtime they all
leave me behind,
alone in the classroom.

They laugh together
go round for tea.
No one ever, ever
asks me.

They play skipping games
I can skip too
but they won't let me
even turn up.

They go round singing
*all join hands*
*if you want to play catch.*
No one catches hold of mine.

I sadly wait till they
come back inside.
Perhaps now they'll talk to me.
It's hard being the teacher.

# MY PETS

I like to make a pet
of a special pupil every year.
Not necessarily one who pleases me.

I don't rush to decide.
After all I've got all year.
There's a lot if thinking to do.

I started it quite a while ago.
Now I've a good collection
of faces I remember, voices that echo.

First there was Fred.
A lovely little lad
but he never finished his work on time.

Then there was Georgina.
She was so helpful, but you know
that can get to be really annoying after a while.

So I started my pets scheme.
Fred makes a super little frog and he's happy
to be staying behind after school for ever with
        me.

Georgina's made a lovely Pekinese,
*adores* having her hair brushed and so handy
when it comes to fetching my slippers.

So who this year?
I rather fancy a cat next.
It's more traditional in my line of hobby.

# NEW START

First day back
everything is new.
New teacher (the one
you thought was so scary
last year), new classroom
(walls all blank waiting for
the new display), new shirt
(the collar stiff and scratchy),
new pencil, rubber, pencil case
(Dad took you to town to choose)
new work (much harder, you'll never
be able to do it). BUT same old kids
some you like and some you don't.
New start. This is the year I'm not
going to be scared any more. Year 6.

# THE STAFF

Miss Linnet is neat and very precise
she flutters her skirts around.
She sweeps along the corridors
thin fingers curled round
her art pad, feet tapping along
in stiletto heels, sharp as tacks.

Mrs Tabby has green eyes.
Be sure they'll find you out.
You may think she is snoozing
curled up in her chair
but one ear is always pricked
to see what you're doing there.

Mr Mastiff's our head.
He's gruff and snappy.
Miss Linnet and Mrs Tabby say
his bark's as bad as his bite.
You'll never get the better of him —
he's always in the right.

# AFTER SCHOOL CINQUAINS

### FOR THE WASH

My socks
Jazzy jumping ones
Stripy frogged and clocked ones
Birthday bright and bobbled ones, now
Sweaty.

### FOUR O'CLOCK SNACK

Sandwich
No butter please
Crusty bread thick cut some cheese
Lettuce tomato mustard please
Great Stuff!

### ON THE TRANSIENCE OF PLEASURE

Hot day
Pink ice lolly
Soft ice-cream inside it
Cool treat melting on my tongue, now
Just stick.

AFTER SCHOOL

Switch on
Spiderman starts
I fight villains and win
Without stirring a fingertip.
Magic!

# BONFIRE NIGHT

Fireworks blossom on
the black sugar paper sky.

The spicy smell of first frost
makes nostrils tingle.

The bonfire burns like a furnace.
My face is as hot as an iron.

My fleece jacket is snuggled
round me to keep me warm.

I write my name in air
with my white hot sparkler.

Before bed, there's hot chocolate,
floating cushions of marshmallow.

# HALLOWE'EN PARTY

We've made a pumpkin lantern
and fixed a candle within.
The apples are floating in a bowl
treacle toffee's cool in the tin.

Toffee apples are gleaming stickily,
stories wait to be shared,
Mum's made a heavy Parkin cake,
our costumes are fully prepared.

It's nearly time for the party
and I'm straining up the lane
to see if anyone's coming —
yes, here's Jennifer and Jane

One is dressed as a devil
in tights and cloak of red.
The other looks like a vampire
as pale as one undead.

Now here's Meeta and Annabel —
a skeleton and a ghoul.
You'd never know so many spooks
went to our school.

There's witches and wizards,
monsters, devils, ghosts and sprites.
Now it's time for stories.
Turn off all the lights!

Now listen while mum tells us
about blood-sucking Loupgaroo,
the story of Janet and Tam Lin
and lots of others too.

Till our eyes droop in the candlelight,
our heads are full of dreams
and it's time for friends to go back home
until next Hallowe'en.

# CHRISTMAS TREE

I
was
chosen
by my family,
picked
out from hundreds
of other trees.
They brought me home and
placed me
where I could be admired.
They decked me
in gaudy jewels and on my arms
outstretched
they draped fine gold vines and garlands.
An angel
sings from my topmost twig, fine songs
of a baby and its mother.
Wrapped boxes
shelter under
my trunk
waiting.

# RECIPE FOR A FESTIVAL

Take some excited people
looking forward
dressed in their best.

Add assorted customs
and memories and tales.
Sift carefully.

Include special food
lovingly made
the old-fashioned way.

Prepare to enjoy yourself.

# RECIPE FOR A BIRTHDAY

### INGREDIENTS:

One clear morning
Birthday paper
Presents bought in secret
Icing sugar
The right number of little candles
A cake to stick them in
People to sing
Friend's faces
All smiles

### METHOD:

Mix together
Simmer all day
Tuck up in bed when done.

# THE CREATION DISCO

First there was nothing
Then rain said 'let there be spring'.
And there was spring.

In the green wet grass
Where nothing had been but blades
Some crocus bubbled.

The daffodils and bluebells
Joined the party. And snakeshead fritillaries
Bent their spotted heads.

The spring disco-danced
All over the sprouting garden
In her best frock.

The party went on until
They were all worn out. Then sun said
'Let there be summer'.

And there was.

# WINTER MORNING

Take one starry night
without cloud blankets.
Sprinkle icing sugar all about.
Leave to set.

Frosted leaves
sugared trees
spider's web appears
marked out in silver pen.

Serve with hats and mitts on,
boots and scarves on.
Scrape silver from the car.
Outside's a big fridge.

By dinner time the sun
you left it to bake in
has licked up all the sugar.
Winter's work's undone.

# WEATHERINGS

The breezes of the spring wake up
and lark about the garden having fun
that's the time that I love most to play
before the weather makes itself too hot.

On sunny summer nights I lie awake
and listen to the stories of the birds
nattering about the worms they've caught
and calling to their young to come to bed.

On windy autumn nights when rain
knocks on the glass and begs to be let in
I snuggle down into my downy quilt
and wait for it to give up hope and leave.

The snow and hail and fog and ice and frost
all come to whiten up the winter time.
The weather makes the magic of the day
and turns my childhood years to memory.

# FINDING MAGIC

Magic's not that stuff on telly,
we all know how that's done.
No, it's the shimmering pink horizon
at the rising of the sun.

It's not some trick with rabbits
popping from a black top hat
No, it's the furry liquefaction
of a sleekly moving cat.

You can keep disappearing elephants
worked by reflective glass
look instead at daisies
prinking in the grass.

Sawing the lady in pieces
or making her disappear
is nothing to the moonlight
reflected in the mere.

There's no trick anywhere like it
nor a more impressive sight
than when the winter's icy wand
magics everywhere snow white

So never mind the conjurer
as he tries to trick your view
think about nature's cleverest trick
that most appeals to you!

# HAIKU FOR THE SEASONS

Who has dropped this purse
On the path spilling copper?
The horse chestnut tree.


In fog, and the road
Stops mid-air — hold your breath, pray —
Oh, the brow of a hill.


Snowdrops for earbobs,
Dress of crocus petal silk,
Spring, the debutante.


Nights of hot honey,
On the bed a single sheet.
When will coolness come?

# FRIENDS

He was a tall black Arab,
she was five years old,
the first black person
she had ever seen.

It was love at first sight.

He was big and gentle,
sat her on his knee,
called her a little lady,
taught her strange new facts.

His list of continents began with Africa.

They were always together.
In his home he was a teacher.
She loved his beautiful skin,
his soft curly hair.

Now she knew the world differently.

Walking in the garden
she only reached his knee,
Her small hand resting
in his huge strong fist.

He sent her postcards for years.

Only later did she know
how her father had
defended him from
people in the street.

How could anyone not love
Nasr Hassan Abbas?
His very name was a poem,
a shelter from any storm,

Now she knew the world differently.

# MY BEST FRIEND

We stand on the riverbank
while he shows me
where trout lie.

He knows the names
of all wild things
in the earth and sky.

He taught me colours
and animal prints,
bought me a kite.

We laugh a lot.
He tells old jokes
to make things right.

We play cards for money —
old pennies he's saved.
He's my best mate.

He buys me chips
in a drippy vinegar bag.
My grandad's great.

# AFTER THE EARTHQUAKE

Whether to cry out in answer to
my father's strangled cries
as he shifts bricks above my head,
or whether to keep silent, holding back
this dust with clamped lips. I lie
sealed in and cannot choose.

If I speak, death will steal my breath
seeping in at the mouth;
if I choose silence he may go away
and weep, and never know how close
my grave or how I longed to answer.

Someone flutes powder from my face.
I feel warm breath. My eyelids move:
their flutter fills my eyes with grit.
Weight lifts from my chest and arms
and inch by inch I live again.

In my father's arms
I cannot find strength to haul up
words from my darkness.

# CHANGE OUR WAYS

I own an orchard
But I won't give you one apple.

I cultivate a beanfield.
I sell you soya at good profit.

I have an education.
I use it to put one over on you.

My shelves are full of books.
I won't teach you to read.

I glory in bright silks to wear.
I give you cast-offs.

I have much to learn.
Will you teach me?

# KENNING MY DAD

He comes home smelling of outside
a bootstamping coat remover.
When he sits at the table
he's a food exterminator
a coffee-consuming pudding praiser.
He's a mountain strider, birdwatcher,
a cheering on at rugby shouter
a dolls house maker, breadbaker,
cooking pasta in the kitchen on Sunday.
He's a vegetable nurturer
digging in the garden in the rain
a leekbringer, soup inventor.
At work he's a computer tapper
brainworker, travelling on a train worker.
at home he's our dad —
a bighugging loudlaughing funloving
daft teasing dad with a prickly face.

# RIDDLE

I hum in the summer kitchen,
a white box of winter. I make
ice while the sun shines. My
light flicks on and off at your
*whim*. In me you hide fruit of
summer, safe from the brown
menace of heat which thieves
its bloom. Water in me is like
the water from mountain pools
cooled in my frosty embrace.
I bring relief from the midday
blistering sun when you clink
my gift of ice cubes in squash.
Cool                    chill.

# HYPOCRITES

Mum and dad go on and on
'Tidy your room', they scream.
I can't see a problem
It's my space to think and dream.
I have a stick collection
and quite a lot of stones
but dad is being sarky
about tyrannosaurus bones.
I keep my clothes in tidy heaps
piled up on the floor
it's really not my look out
that dad can't open the door.
I have a lot of hobbies
and I need this stuff that's here.
You shouldn't stifle genius
when it might appear.

Mum and dad are out today
so I crept into their room.
They don't practise what they preach —
it's like a mummy's tomb.
Her dressing table's scattered
with jewellery of all kinds.
Dad's chest of drawers is groaning
with all his fossil finds.
Their clothes are in a tangle

their shoes are in a heap
their books lie piled up on the floor
with magazines knee deep.
The bed is left all rumpled.
the sheets are less than clean
but I can't say a word to them
or they'll find out where I've been!

# AFTER THE MATCH

Did yer see the other team?
Thee all 'ad one leg,
'ands tied behind their backs.
Ah've seen better schoolboys round our way
kickin' ball in't street.
Their kits were rubbish:
thee didn't even look the part,
more like rag and bone men.
Feller who trained 'em should ha'
taught 'em to play football
not nancy around with the ball
like ballet dancers.
An' another thing.
That ref was blind
Or thee'd never ha' won.

# LITTLE HOUSES

Houses I have made and loved:
three umbrellas in the garden
a blanket on the floor
make a pavilion for one princess.

A draped sheet, a clothes-horse
becomes a ridge tent
hideaway on rainy days,
camping in the house.

Bigger houses take longer.
One we lived in for three days,
and even kept the rain out,
boasted a corrugated iron roof.

There were three rooms,
mattresses on the floor.
At night our mothers
wondered who we were.